Stan Lee
Writer & Creator

by Sue Hamilton

Visit us at
www.abdopublishing.com

Published by ABDO Publishing Company, 4940 Viking Drive, Suite 622, Edina, Minnesota
55435. Copyright ©2007 by Abdo Consulting Group, Inc. International copyrights reserved
in all countries. No part of this book may be reproduced in any form without written
permission from the publisher. ABDO & Daughters™ is a trademark and logo of ABDO
Publishing Company.

Printed in the United States.

Editor: John Hamilton
Graphic Design: Sue Hamilton
Cover Design: Neil Klinepier
Cover Illustration: Stan Lee, Corbis
Interior Photos and Illustrations: pp 1 - 32 All Marvel comic book character and cover
images used with permission from Marvel Entertainment, Inc., p 1 Stan Lee, Corbis;
p 5 Lieber family, courtesy Stan Lee; p 6 Eleanor Roosevelt, Getty Images; p 7 Stanley
Lieber on bike, courtesy Stan Lee; p 10 *Honolulu Star-Bulletin*, Getty Images; p 10 USS
Arizona burning, Digital Stock; p 11 Stan Lee in uniform, courtesy Stan Lee; p 13 Stan and
Joanie Lee, courtesy Stan Lee; p 15 Code Authority Charles F. Murphy, Corbis; p 17 Stan
Lee at work, courtesy Stan Lee; p 19 Stan Lee, courtesy Stan Lee; p 23 Health, Education,
and Welfare Seal, National Archives and Records Administration, Harry S. Truman Library;
p 24 Stan Lee and Nicholas Hammond, Getty Images; p 25 Incredible Hulk, Getty Images;
p 26 X-Men Movie Poster, courtesy 20th Century Fox; p 27 Stan Lee, Getty Images;
p 28 Stan Lee, Getty Images; p 29 Stan Lee, Getty Images; p 31 Stan Lee, courtesy Stan Lee.

Library of Congress Cataloging-in-Publication Data

Hamilton, Sue L., 1959-
  Stan Lee / Sue Hamilton.
    p. cm. -- (Comic book creators)
  Includes index.
  ISBN-13: 978-1-59928-301-2
  ISBN-10: 1-59928-301-8
  1. Lee, Stan--Juvenile literature. 2. Cartoonists--United States--Biography--Juvenile
literature. I. Title. II. Series: Hamilton, Sue L., 1959- Comic book creators.

PN6727.L39Z66 2007
741.5092--dc22
  [B]
                            2005035430

Contents

Stan "The Man" Lee 4

Sometimes, It's Who You Know 6

Wonder Writer 8

Army Man 10

Model Marries The Man 12

The Comics Code Authority 14

The Wonderful Web They Wove 16

Fun With Superheroes 18

Fantastic Fan Clubs 20

The Marvel Method 22

Publisher, Promoter, & Positive Influence 24

Stan "The Chairman" 26

POW! Entertainment 28

Glossary 30

Index 32

Stan "The Man" Lee

Spider-Man. X-Men. The Incredible Hulk. Daredevil. The Fantastic Four. Iron Man. The Avengers. Silver Surfer. Dr. Strange. Nick Fury. Throughout the 20th century, millions of kids and adults grew up reading stories created by Stan "The Man" Lee. Born Stanley Martin Lieber on December 28, 1922, Stan grew up to be the creator, co-creator, and writer for some of the most famous superheroes of all time.

Stan was raised in New York City. Not surprisingly, many of his stories took place in the Big Apple. Stan practiced the old rule that the best way to write is to write about things you know. Stan knew New York.

His parents, Jack and Celia Lieber, came to the United States from Romania. They were immigrants. They weren't rich, and they weren't writers. They were, however, very hard working. As a boy, Stan learned the importance of work. He skipped grades in school so he could graduate early. Stan then began working to get money for the family. His family faced rough years during the Great Depression, when there were few jobs and little money.

When he wasn't working, Stan loved to go to the movies. He also loved to read. Soon, he began writing and illustrating his own stories. It was the start of something that would shape his life, and the lives of millions of comic book readers around the world.

Above: The Lieber family, Stan at far left, age 10, in New York City.

Sometimes, It's Who You Know

In 1931, when Stan was nine, his brother Larry was born. Another person in the family meant even more pressure for the young man to keep working hard. Like most kids, Stan held many different jobs in his youth. While an usher at a movie theater, he once escorted First Lady Eleanor Roosevelt to her seat. Of course, in his effort to be as professional as possible, he walked with excellent posture, eyes straight ahead, leading the way. Suddenly, he tripped over someone's feet and fell flat on his face. Mrs. Roosevelt helped him up and asked if he was okay. He was fine, but as he puts it, "It wasn't my proudest moment."

Above: First Lady Eleanor Roosevelt, 1933.

Stan also sold subscriptions to the *New York Times* newspaper. He delivered sandwiches for a drugstore. He worked as an actor (which he loved and still loves today), but his parts paid very little and he had to quit. He even worked as an office boy at a trouser manufacturer.

Stan continued writing. He entered a local newspaper's contest in which he had to write "The Biggest News of the Week." After winning three weeks in a row, the newspaper editor asked him to stop submitting articles so someone else could win for a change.

Left: Stan Lee on his bike, age 12.

When Stan graduated from high school, he needed a "real" job. That's where his Uncle Robbie came in. Robbie Solomon worked for a New York publisher, and they needed a "gopher" (someone to "go-for" this and that). Stan got the job.

But family connections didn't stop with Uncle Robbie. Martin Goodman, who was married to Stan's cousin Jean, owned Western Fiction Publishing. Stan and Goodman knew of each other, but they hadn't spent much time together. However, this connection would eventually give Stan a start on his life's work.

Wonder Writer

Western Fiction Publishing printed cheap pulp magazines such as *Star Detective, Uncanny Stories*, and *Mystery Tales*. These were the forerunners of comic books. When comics started to become popular, Martin Goodman decided to produce these cheap publications, printing them under the name of Timely Publications. The first comic book came out in October 1939. It was simply called *Marvel Comics* #1. At that time, nobody knew that "Marvel" would eventually become the name of the company.

Superheroes soon became super-sellers. From Timely Publications came such comic books as *The Sub-Mariner*, created by Bill Everett, and *The Human Torch*, by Carl Burgos. One big success was *Captain America*, by Joe Simon and Jack Kirby.

Editor Joe Simon and Jack Kirby, the staff artist, needed help. Luckily, they knew that Stan could write. They also knew he was a hard worker. Stan may have been only 17 years old, but suddenly he found himself writing his first comic book story: "Captain America Foils the Traitor's Revenge," published in May 1941, in *Captain America* #3.

Believing that someday he'd earn a living writing novels, Stan decided to write comic books under a pseudonym. He wanted to save his real name, Stanley Lieber, for his first book. So, he took his first name, broke it in half, and changed the "y" to an extra "e." Thus was born, "Stan Lee."

Stan later wrote many stories for Timely, including Westerns, mysteries, science fiction, horror, and even romance. To make it look as though there were more than one person writing for the company, he created many other pen names: S.T. Anley, Stan Martin, and Neel Nats (look at it backwards).

Above: Star Detective, a pulp magazine published by Martin Goodman. *The Sub-Mariner,* one of Timely Publications' first comic books, created by Bill Everett. Stan Lee's first published story was in *Captain America #3,* issue date May 1941.

Army Man

Top Left:
Front page of the *Honolulu Star-Bulletin*, December 8, 1941.

Top Right:
USS *Arizona* burning after the Japanese attack on Pearl Harbor.

On December 7, 1941, the Imperial Japanese Navy bombed the headquarters of the U.S. Navy Pacific Fleet at Pearl Harbor in Oahu, Hawaii. World War II had begun.

In 1942, Stan enlisted in the U.S. Army. He began his tour of duty at Fort Monmouth, New Jersey. It was very cold that winter. One night after guard duty in the freezing wind, Stan said that he ran back to the barracks and stood so close to the heater that he started his uniform on fire, turning himself into a real-life Human Torch! Luckily, he was fine.

After basic training, the young man was in for a surprise. When the Army learned Stan was a writer, he received orders to return to New York and begin writing for the Signal Corps' Training Film Division. He had the great honor of being one of only nine men in the entire U.S. Army to be classified as a "playwright."

Stan spent his time working on such simple topics as *Organizing a Footlocker.* He was also given many topics about which he knew absolutely nothing. Stan said, "I've never forgotten the title of this assignment: *The Nomenclature and Operation of a 16mm Eyemo Camera Under Combat Conditions.* I got the Army texts and made them simpler, so soldiers could understand them faster and better." Never one to waste time, Stan turned in his work quicker than everyone else. In fact, he was told to slow down; he was making everyone else look bad!

Above: Stan Lee in uniform, circa 1943.

During the war years, comic books became so popular that approximately 25 million copies were sold each month. However, Timely Publications found themselves lacking writers, since so many had joined the military. Stan found this out and started writing comics during his off-duty time. Every Friday he'd receive an outline from New York. By Monday he'd mail a finished story back to the publisher.

When Sergeant Stanley Lieber was honorably discharged from the Army in 1945, he had produced not only hundreds of Army films and posters, but hundreds of comic book stories as well.

Model Marries The Man

After World War II ended, Stan returned to Timely Publications and picked up where he'd never actually left off. Whatever topic was popular, Stan's flying fingers pounded out the stories on his typewriter. He wrote crime comics such as *Official True Crime Cases* and *Private Eye*. He produced romances for girls to read, such as *Millie the Model* and *The Blonde Phantom*. He even wrote Westerns such as *Black Rider*. (Stan didn't own a horse, but he did enjoy riding in New York's Central Park, which was allowed at the time.) Then war comics became the "in" thing, and Stan found himself producing stories for *Combat Kelly* and *Battle Brady*.

Then, in 1947, another family member made a huge impact on Stan's life. This time, a cousin asked Stan to go to a modeling agency to meet a friend of his named Betty. Stan went to the agency, but instead of Betty, he met Joan Boocock, a beautiful woman who modeled hats.

Stan and Joanie soon fell in love. On December 5, 1947, they were married in Reno, Nevada. Of course, then Stan had to bring his new wife back to New York to meet his family. Luckily for him, both his mother and father loved Joanie.

The couple settled down. Three years later they had a baby, Joan Celia. Stan continued writing comic book stories to pay the bills.

Above: Stan and Joanie Lee in the 1950s.
Facing Page: The September 1948 issue of *The Blonde Phantom* was edited by Stan Lee.

The Comics Code Authority

Millions of kids loved reading comic books in the late 1940s and 1950s. Today some call it the "Golden Age" of comics. But there were many people who thought all comics were less than the ideal reading material—in fact, many people thought comics were trash.

Stan was well aware of this prejudice against comics. When asked what he did for a job, he said he was a "writer." He didn't like the way people reacted when he told them he wrote comic books for a living. It seemed odd that huge numbers of Americans spent their money buying these printed adventures, and yet a few outspoken people totally hated the cheap fiction.

Were comic books ruining America's youth? In 1954, the Comics Magazine Association of America was formed. Every company that published comics had to be a part of this association. Every story written had to be submitted to the Comics Code Authority (CCA) for its approval. Every comic book story published in the United States had to have the Comics Code Authority seal of approval.

There were many rules the comic creators had to follow. Crimes and criminals had to be shown as "bad." Police had to be depicted as "good." There was no middle ground. No comic book could be published with the words "horror" or "terror" in its title. Comic book publishers agreed to follow these rules, and all the other CCA guidelines.

Was this censorship? Yes, but this was the way it had to be if the publishers wanted to stay in business. Said Stan Lee,

Above: In a press conference on December 28, 1954, Code Administrator Charles F. Murphy shows the changes made to a comic book character before it was approved by the Comics Code Authority.

"We didn't have much trouble with this. Ninety-nine out of 100 comics would go through without any problem. It held things up a day or two, while they read the book, but we just built it into the production schedule."

Still, Stan was more and more embarrassed to be a part of the comic book industry. He wondered if perhaps the time had come to move on.

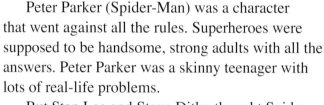

The Wonderful Web They Wove

Timely Publications had changed its name and was now Atlas Publishing. Throughout the last half of the 1950s, the emphasis in comics was on science fiction, BEMs (bug-eyed monsters), and funny animals. These all passed the Comics Code.

By 1962, Stan had worked for Martin Goodman for more than 20 years. Stan felt that Goodman always wanted to follow what was popular, instead of creating new material.

Stan's wife Joan advised him to create whatever character he wanted. If Stan was really going to leave comic books, he might as well go out doing something he wanted. So what if he got fired? He was probably going to leave anyway. So, together with artist Steve Ditko, Stan created a teenage superhero based on the qualities of an arachnid: Spider-Man.

Peter Parker (Spider-Man) was a character that went against all the rules. Superheroes were supposed to be handsome, strong adults with all the answers. Peter Parker was a skinny teenager with lots of real-life problems.

But Stan Lee and Steve Ditko thought Spider-Man would appeal to many normal, everyday people. They brought the first Spider-Man to press by introducing him in the 1962 comic book *Amazing Fantasy.* This was to be the last issue, and nobody really cared what went into the last issue of a comic book series.

The rest is history: Spider-Man was a sell-out. Stan and Ditko's creation got his own magazine in 1963. Atlas became Marvel Comics, and the stage was set for superheroes once again.

Above: Stan Lee at work in his office in the 1950s.
Facing page: Marvel Comics *Amazing Fantasy* Issue #15, the first time Spider-Man is introduced.

Fun With Superheroes

I n the 1960s, Stan Lee and the talented artists of Marvel Comics (who now included Stan's younger brother, Larry Lieber) introduced dozens of new characters. Spider-Man and the other new characters formed the center of the "Marvel Universe." Being part of a comic book universe was exciting, and Stan was at the center of everything. He was having super fun with superheroes.

Many of the Marvel Universe characters were "created" as a result of cosmic rays or radioactivity:

- Spider-Man (Peter Parker) was bitten by a radioactive spider.

- The Fantastic Four (created by Stan and artist Jack Kirby) were on a spaceship bombarded by cosmic rays, which created: Mr. Fantastic (Dr. Reed Richards), who had an elastic body; Invisible Girl (Susan Storm); Human Torch (Johnny Storm); and The Thing (Benjamin Grimm), who was a rock-like beast with incredible strength.

- The Incredible Hulk (Bruce Banner), who was a type of Dr. Jekyll/Mr. Hyde character, was created from exposure to gamma rays.

Above: The universal symbol for radioactivity.

Top Left: A panel from *Fantastic Four* Issue #1, August 1961.
Bottom Left: The Incredible Hulk Issue #1, May 1962.

18

Stan and the Marvel creators also searched for other reasons for their characters' existence:

• They wanted a hero who was stronger and bigger than The Hulk. Only a god-like character fit the bill. Stan, Larry Lieber, and Jack Kirby turned to Norse mythology to create The Mighty Thor, the legendary God of Thunder.

• Wealthy industrialist and inventor Tony Stark turned into Iron Man when he wore his iron costume.

• X-Men were "mutants"—people born with special powers. Stan wanted them to be called "The Mutants." However, his boss, Martin Goodman, thought this was too complicated a word for their readers. "X-Men" came from the idea that each of the characters had some sort of "extra" superpower that normal people didn't possess.

Above Top: The Mighty Thor character with his hammer.
Above Right: Iron Man in his suit.
Above Left: The X-Men Issue #1, September 1963.
Right: Stan Lee, circa 1950s.

Fantastic Fan Clubs

"Like costumed heroes? Confidentially, we in the comic mag business refer to them as 'Long Underwear Characters!'"

Stan made friends for life with his constant attention to readers and their opinions. He communicated regularly with comic book fans. He kept his writing personal and he listened to the fans. He made it a point of telling readers a little about the "secrets" of the comic book industry. He told people about the artists and writers.

Stan loved alliteration, a series of similar sounds. It helped him remember all his characters: Peter Parker; Reed Richards; Susan Storm; Bruce Banner. It didn't stop with the characters—he created names for his writers, artists, and inkers, too: "Sturdy" Stevey Ditko; Jack "King" Kirby; "Jazzy" Johnny Romita; "Adorable Artie" Simek; "Fabulous Flo" Steinberg; "Big John" Buscema. He even had a nickname for his publisher: "Merry" Marty Goodman.

When his column, "Stan's Soapbox," or the "Bullpen Bulletins," or "Letters to the Editor" pages were printed, Stan never signed anything as "The Editor." He was himself: Stan Lee. He didn't sign his letters as "Sincerely," either. He ended his notes with: "'Nuff Said," or "Hang Loose." That is, until the competition started doing the same thing. He wanted to come up with his own closing that no one would copy.

Below: A MMMS packet.

So was born: "Excelsior!" In Old English, it means "Upward and Onward to Greater Glory!" No one else used that.

Stan wanted fans to feel they were a part of the Marvel family. He listened and respected the fans. When they said they didn't like something, he often agreed with them and promised to do better on the next issue. Who wouldn't feel great about having a team of professional comic book writers and artists agree with their point of view? Once, Stan was so honest that he actually wrote on the cover of a comic book that he didn't think it was the best comic they'd done, but please buy it. They'd do better next month. Fans bought it!

Stan even created a fan club: the MMMS. Fans had to guess what the initials meant. Months later came the answer: Merry Marvel Marching Society. Of course, Stan couldn't send out a mere membership card—he had to have something unique. So, he and several Marvel artists recorded a "bullpen session." MMMS members received the five-minute record, and yes, they did get a membership card and a beautiful pin.

High costs ended the MMMS. Later, Stan tried again and created FOOM (Friends of ol' Marvel). That ended, too. Then Stan created "No-Prize" Winners for anyone finding a misspelling or other error in one of Marvel's comic books. It was an empty envelope that said: "CONGRATULATIONS! This envelope contains a genuine Marvel Comics No-Prize, which you have just won!" Decades later, people still ask Stan to autograph their MMMS, FOOM, and "No-Prize" materials. Stan had indeed made friends for life.

ITEM: We've received a zillion letters (wouldja believe a couple?) asking us to have Our Leader do an editorial on this page each ish, in order to bring the Marvel Message to all True Believers! Hence, in obvious obeisance to thy slightest wishes, O Keepers of the Flame, we hereby inaugurate a forensic new feature, to be known forevermore as:

STAN'S SOAPBOX!

Hang loose, heroes! Now that I've got your ear, I'm not lettin' go! Our first tintinnabulating topic is gonna be: "The Marvel Philosophy." Whenever I get together with any of you frantic ones, the first question posed is usually "What are you fellas really trying to DO in your mags? What message are you pushin'? Is the whole Marvel series just a big put-on, or are you trying to TELL us something? Are you actually serious about your characters—do you really believe in 'em—? Etc." Well, just between us, we believe in our cavortin' characters a lot more than we believe in some people we know, and we do have a motive—a purpose—behind our mags! That purpose is, plain and simple — to entertain you! We think we've found the best formula of all—we merely create the type of fanciful yarns that we ourselves enjoy—and, if we like 'em, you oughtta like 'em, too; after all, you're our kinda people! Now then, in the process of providing off-beat entertainment, if we can also do our bit to advance the cause of intellectualism, humanitarianism, and mutual understanding...and to toss a little swingin' satire at you in the process . . . that won't break our collective heart one tiny bit! That's it, pussycat! Thanks for listenin'!

THE WRAP-UP: That sinks it for now, frantic one. But, before we cut out, we wanna remind you to drop Stan a line and tell him what you'd like him to talk about on this page each month. Otherwise, he may not be able to think of a thing to say. (That'll be the day!) So, till we make the scene together again, face front, hang loose, and be good to each other. The human race may not be perfect, but it's the only one we've got! 'Nuff said!

Above: A "Stan's Soapbox" column.

The Marvel Method

C omic books are a merging of written and artistic
talents. Although a writer, Stan always pointed out
how important the artists were in producing comic
books. He may have had the ideas, but the artists used their art
to grow and develop characters and stories. So much emphasis
was placed in the hands of the artists that he called them "co-
creators." (For example, Steve Ditko was the co-creator of
Spider-Man.)

As busy as Stan was as a writer, his job at Marvel called
for him to do much more. He was an editor who read and
corrected other people's stories. He assigned work to artists.
He made sure deadlines were met, and he worked on creating
new ideas and characters. His busy schedule caused what
became known as the "Marvel Method."

If Stan was too busy finishing one project, but another one
needed to get started, he would give a very basic outline to
the artist: "Spider-Man is battling the Green Goblin. Spidey
loses the first fight, but goes on to beat Gobby at the top of a
skyscraper." The artist would then draw the panels, and Stan
would fill in the exact words later. Because all of Marvel's
artists were such excellent visual storytellers, the Marvel
Method worked perfectly. Everyone was kept busy, and Stan
wasn't writing day and night. He did, however, take on one
specific writing assignment himself.

In 1971, Stan was asked to serve his government again. The United States Office of Health, Education, and Welfare (renamed in 1979 to Department of Health & Human Services) called and asked him to write an anti-drug message into one of his comic books. Naturally, Stan agreed, and he created a three-part series where one of Spider-Man's friends overdosed on drugs.

What made this government-requested, anti-drug comic book special was that when Stan submitted it to the Comics Code Authority, they wouldn't approve it—it showed someone using drugs. Comics weren't allowed to show anything about drugs, not even their horrible effects.

Stan figured that the U.S. government was above the Comics Code Authority, and published the series without the Code's seal of approval. Stan received hundreds of letters from schools, religious leaders, parents, and anti-drug organizations praising *The Amazing Spider-Man* Issues #96-98. The Code was changed afterwards, allowing for anti-drug themes.

Above Left: The United States Department of Health, Education, and Welfare Seal.
Above Center: The Comics Code Authority seal, usually placed on an approved comic book's cover in the upper right corner.
Above: Marvel Comics' *The Amazing Spider-Man* Issues #96-98, published in 1971 without the Comics Code Authority approval.

Publisher, Promoter, & Positive Influence

In the 1970s, publisher Martin Goodman retired. Stan gave up his role as editor-in-chief and took over as publisher of Marvel. What does a publisher do? Something that Stan loved: he promoted Marvel Comics!

Stan traveled worldwide, speaking to crowds about Marvel. "Frankly," said Stan, "I wanted to be an actor. Being able to lecture and make speeches is the closest thing to being an actor without being an actor."

Above: Stan Lee talks to Nicholas Hammond, the actor who played Peter Parker/Spider-Man on the television series *The Amazing Spider-Man,* July 6, 1978.

By now, Stan "The Man" Lee was very famous. He traveled all over Europe, Japan, and even China. "In Beijing," said Stan, "they gave me the honorary title of 'Exhaulted Creator.' I was told that I was the only American—not a politician—who had ever spoken in the Great Hall of the People there."

Stan vividly remembers his trip to Mexico City. "I had six bodyguards, two in front, two in back and one on either side. There were thousands of people . . . As I started walking, the crowd began to part like Moses parting the Red Sea. All these people were shouting, 'Olé, Stan Lee!' One of the guards turned to me and said if I ran for president, I'd be elected in a second!"

The Marvel Universe had become huge. There were animated TV shows (*The Fantastic Four, Spider-Man, Dr. Strange,* and *Captain America*), live-action shows (*Spider-Man* and *The Incredible Hulk*), and a Spider-Man newspaper strip, written and inked by Stan and his brother, Larry Lieber. This continues to be published nearly 30 years later,

Then came Marvel Productions. It was in 1986 that Marvel Comics turned 25 years old and was sold to New World Entertainment. Stan and his family made the move to Hollywood. Stan now worked, technically, for a company other than Marvel. He had to get used to changing employers. Only two years later Stan began working for Marvel Films. Marvel Films was created after Ron Perelman purchased New World Entertainment.

Then, in the 1990s, comic book sales took a downturn when the collecting craze passed. Suddenly, Marvel was in trouble.

Right: Lou Ferrigno as The Hulk holds actress Laurie Prange in a 1980 photo from the television series, *The Incredible Hulk.*

Stan "The Chairman"

In 1998, Marvel filed for bankruptcy. It looked like Stan might actually be out of a job. But, once again, Marvel survived and he was given the title "Chairman Emeritus." Basically, that meant he could do whatever projects he wanted to do. However, everything in Marvel was pretty much taken care of.

Below: X-Men movie poster.

Stan Lee Media came next. Together with partner Peter Paul, and a large creative staff, Stan developed "webisodes" on the Internet. Although the company started out very well, something went incredibly bad. Peter Paul left the country and the company was forced to close down.

It might have been a horrible ending to a life-long career, but Stan had other things going on, including huge big-screen successes. In 2000, 20th Century Fox released the feature film *X-Men*, starring Hugh Jackman and Patrick Stewart. In 2002, came Columbia Pictures' *Spider-Man*, starring Tobey Maguire, Kirsten Dunst, and Willem Dafoe. In 2003, Universal released *The Hulk*. And in 2004, came *Daredevil,* with Ben Affleck, and *Spider-Man 2,* which won an Oscar for Special Effects.

Above: Stan Lee at the premiere of *Spider-Man 2*, June 2004.

POW! Entertainment

In 2002, Stan became Chief Creative Officer for POW! Entertainment. POW stands for "Purveyors of Wonder!" The job allowed him to do what he loves most: writing, acting, and working on comics, cartoons, and movies. He continues to stay in touch with his fans, too. "I'm very compulsive and I try to answer every message and letter I get. I spend hours answering."

After his many years of success, Stan became proud to tell people he was a comic book writer. And after all those years, which of his characters was his favorite? Said Stan, "Whichever one I happened to be writing at the time, because I used to get totally enmeshed in each character and story when I wrote them. But, if my very life depended on picking one now, I'd have to say Spider-Man because he became the most famous and, whenever people introduce me to someone, they inevitably say, 'This is Stan Lee, the creator of Spider-Man.'"

Right: Stan Lee in front of a painting showing himself and several Marvel characters.

Above: Stan Lee in his office on June 18, 2004.

Glossary

BANKRUPTCY

When a company or person has more bills than ability to pay, the "debtor" may file bankruptcy in court. The court will then arrange for part of the owed money to be paid back by having the debtor sell items that they own.

BULLPEN SESSION

When several members of the Marvel publishing staff, especially writers and artists, get together to share ideas.

CENSORSHIP

The control of what is written or spoken by a central authority, often a government or large group of outspoken individuals.

CO-CREATOR

A person working with another person to make up a comic book character. Especially in the comic book area, often a writer and an artist work together to develop characters' stories, as well as their look, outfit, and special abilities.

COMICS CODE AUTHORITY (CAA)

Established in 1954 as a way for comic book publishers to deal with parents' concerns about the effects of crime and horror comics on kids. Every comic book published required the CCA's seal of approval, and had to follow a strict set of guidelines. The Code is still in use today, although not all comic books are published with the CCA seal.

CREATOR

A person who thinks up the personality, physical look, and special skills of a comic book character.

DEADLINES

When a job or project must be completed. Usually an amount of time or specific date.

Above: Stan Lee writing in the 1950s.

GREAT DEPRESSION
A time in American history, beginning in 1929 and lasting for several years, when the stock market crashed, which resulted in business failures across the country and the loss of jobs for millions of people.

ILLUSTRATE
To add a piece of art to a printed story. The art may be a drawing, painting, or photo.

IMMIGRANTS
People who move from one country to another, taking the new country as their home.

PREJUDICE
A negative opinion often formed without knowing all the facts.

PSEUDONYM
A fake name often used by writers and artists who do not want to use their real name for various reasons. Also called a "pen name."

PULP MAGAZINES
A nickname for fiction magazines published on the cheapest possible paper made from wood pulp. Also called "the pulps."

ROMANIA
A country in the southeastern part of Central Europe, roughly the size of Oregon.

SUPERHEROES
Characters, often human, but also sometimes aliens or mythological beings, who develop or have special skills that give them superhuman powers. These characters use their powers for good, helping and protecting people.

WEBISODES
Short audio or video presentations on the World Wide Web, which may advertise a product or announce a news event or other information.

WORLD WAR II
A war that was fought from 1939 to 1945, involving countries around the world. The United States entered the war after Japan's bombing of the American naval base at Pearl Harbor, in Oahu, Hawaii, on December 7, 1941.

Index

A

Affleck, Ben 26
Amazing Fantasy 16
Amazing Spider-Man
(newspaper strip) 25
Amazing Spider-Man, The,
Issues #96-98 23
Anley, S.T. 8
Atlas Publishing 16
Avengers 4

B

Banner, Bruce 18, 20
Battle Brady 12
Beijing, China 25
"Biggest News of the Week,
The" 6
Black Rider 12
Blonde Phantom, The 12
Boocock, Joan 12
"Bullpen Bulletins" 20
Burgos, Carl 8
Buscema, John 20

C

Captain America 8
Captain America (animated
TV show) 25
"Captain America Foils the
Traitor's Revenge" 8
Central Park 12
China 25
Columbia Pictures 26
Combat Kelly 12
Comics Code Authority
(CCA) 14, 16, 23
Comics Magazine
Association of America
14

D

Dafoe, Willem 26
Daredevil 4
Daredevil (film) 26
Department of Health &
Human Services 23
Ditko, Steve 16, 20, 22
Dunst, Kirsten 26

E

Europe 25
Everett, Bill 8
Excelsior! 21

F

Fantastic Four 4, 18
Fantastic Four, The
(animated TV show) 25
Fantastic, Mr. 18
Fort Monmouth, NJ 10
Friends of ol' Marvel
(FOOM) 21
Fury, Nick 4

G

God of Thunder 19
Golden Age of Comics 14
Goodman, Jean 7
Goodman, Martin 7, 8, 16,
19, 20, 24
Great Depression 4
Great Hall of the People
25
Green Goblin 22
Grimm, Benjamin 18

H

Hollywood, CA 25
Hulk *(see Incredible Hulk)*
Hulk, The (film) 26
Human Torch 10, 18
Human Torch, The 8
Hyde, Mr. 18

I

Imperial Japanese Navy
10
Incredible Hulk 4, 18, 19
Incredible Hulk, The (live
action TV show) 25
Invisible Girl 18
Iron Man 4, 19

J

Jackman, Hugh 26
Japan 25
Jekyll, Dr. 18

K

Kirby, Jack 8, 18, 19, 20

L

Lee, Joan 12, 16
Lee, Joan Celia 12
Lee, Stan 4, 6, 7, 8, 10, 11,
12, 14, 15, 16, 18, 19,
20, 21, 22, 23, 24, 25,
26, 28
"Letters to the Editor" 20
Lieber, Celia 4
Lieber, Jack 4
Lieber, Larry 6, 18, 19, 25
Lieber, Stanley Martin 4,
6, 7, 8, 10, 11

M

Maguire, Tobey 26
Martin, Stan 8
Marvel Comics 8, 16, 18,
19, 21, 22, 24, 25, 26
Marvel Comics #1 8
Marvel Films 25
Marvel Method 22
Marvel Productions 25
Marvel Universe 18, 25
Merry Marvel Marching
Society (MMMS) 21
Mexico City, Mexico 25
Mighty Thor, The 19
Millie the Model 12
Moses 25
Mutants, The 19
Mystery Tales 8

N

Nats, Neel 8
New World Entertainment
25
New York, NY 4, 7, 11, 12
New York Times 6
*Nomenclature and
Operation of a 16mm
Eyemo Camera Under
Combat Conditions,
The* 11
"No-Prize" Winners 21

O

Oahu, Hawaii 10
Office of Health, Education,
and Welfare 23
Official True Crime Cases
12
Organizing a Footlocker 11
Oscar 26

P

Pacific Fleet, U.S. Navy 10
Parker, Peter 16, 18, 20
Paul, Peter 26
Pearl Harbor 10
Perelman, Ron 25
POW! Entertainment 26
Private Eye 12
Purveyors of Wonder! 26

R

Red Sea 25
Reno, NV 12
Richards, Reed 18, 20

Romania 4
Romita, John 20
Roosevelt, Eleanor 6

S

seal of approval, CCA
14, 23
Signal Corps, U.S.
Army 11
Silver Surfer 4
Simek, Artie 20
Simon, Joe 8
Solomon, Robbie 7
Spider-Man 4, 16, 18,
22, 23, 28
Spider-Man (animated TV
show) 25
Spider-Man (film) 26
Spider-Man (live action TV
show) 25
Spider-Man 2 (film) 26
Stan Lee Media 26
"Stan's Soapbox" 20, 21
Star Detective Magazine 8
Stark, Tony 19
Steinberg, Flo 20
Stewart, Patrick 26
Storm, Johnny 18
Storm, Susan 18, 20
Strange, Dr. 4
Strange, Dr. (animated TV
show) 25
Sub-Mariner, The 8

T

Thing, The 18
Timely Publications 8, 11,
12, 16
Training Film Division,
Signal Corps 11
20th Century Fox 26

U

Uncanny Stories 8
United States 4, 14, 23
United States Army 10, 11
United States Navy 10
Universal Pictures 26

W

Western Fiction Publishing
7, 8
World War II 10, 12

X

X-Men 4, 19
X-Men (film) 26